GW00857489

African Animals

Elizabeth Nonweiler

raintree

dik-dik

okapi

red colobus

jackal

baboon

addax

mamba

mandrill

fennec fox

forest hog

sun squirrel

wildebeest

Interesting facts about the pictures

page 2: **Dik-diks** are small – about 30 centimetres tall. They eat leaves and berries. If a dik-dik sees another animal that might kill it, it makes a call that sounds like "dik-dik" to warn others of danger.

page 3: **Okapis** are sometimes called zebra giraffes. They have very long tongues for cleaning their ears and eyelids. They live in the rainforest and eat leaves and other parts of plants.

page 4: **Red colobus** monkeys live in troops. They look after each other, especially their babies, but sometimes they quarrel and fight. Chimpanzees like to hunt and eat them.

page 5: **Jackals** are like wild dogs. They eat whatever they can get, including small mammals, plants and even poisonous snakes. They can run very fast for a long time and often hunt at night.

page 6: **Baboons** communicate with each other by waving, grunting, smacking their lips, screaming or making faces. Each sound or action means something different.

page 7: **Addax** have long twisted horns. They live in herds of up to 20 members in the Sahara Desert. They can survive without water for a long time. The oldest female in the herd leads them.

page 8: **Mambas** are long snakes. They can move very fast to get away from animals or people if they think they are in danger. If they cannot get away they may bite. Their bite is very poisonous.

page 9: **Mandrills** are the largest monkeys in the world. They live with hundreds of other mandrills in forests and climb high up in trees. They can roar loudly.

page 10: **Fennec foxes** are like very small dogs. They live in the desert and can get enough water from their food without drinking. They can jump up to 60 centimetres high and 120 centimetres forwards.

page 11: **Forest hogs** like to live in wet forests. They have long black bristles and are very heavy, weighing up to 275 kilograms. Mother hogs make nests of grass and branches for their babies. The babies are called piglets.

page 12: **Sun squirrels** are long, thin and lightweight, so they can easily move fast through trees. They like to lie in the sun on tree branches. They spend most of their time alone.

page 13: **Wildebeests** live in herds on open plains and eat grass. Lions, crocodiles and other animals like to eat them. When they are attacked they run very fast. They stay together to protect each other.

Letter-sound correspondences

Level 1 books cover the following letter-sound correspondences.
Letter-sound correspondences highlighted in green can be found
in this book.

<u>a</u>nt	<u>b</u>ig	<u>c</u>at	<u>d</u>og	<u>e</u>gg	fish	<u>g</u>et	<u>h</u>ot	<u>i</u>t
<u>j</u>et	<u>k</u>ey	<u>l</u>et	<u>m</u>an	<u>n</u>ut	<u>o</u>ff	<u>p</u>an	<u>qu</u>een	<u>r</u>un
<u>s</u>un	<u>t</u>ap	<u>u</u>p	**<u>v</u>an**	<u>w</u>et	bo<u>x</u>	**<u>y</u>es**	**<u>z</u>oo**	

du**ck**	fi**sh**	**ch**ips	si**ng**	**th**in **th**is	k**ee**p	l**oo**k m**oo**n	**ar**t	c**or**n